Ken Ham has provided an incredibly urgent, clear and compelling resource that will help Christians everywhere to be strong in their faith and able to speak Gospel truth in today's culture. As a pastor I am very excited to have this book as I know it will help our church in its mission to reach our generation for Christ.

Dr. Brad Jurkovich
Senior Pastor, First Baptist Church, Bossier City, LA

Western culture is consistently moving further and further from an understanding of the gospel of Jesus Christ. In large part, this is due to the fact that many today do not have a foundational trust of the Bible. In *Gospel Reset*, Ken Ham builds the case for presenting the gospel from Genesis to reach this current generation. Every follower of Christ will benefit from reading this book.

Robby Gallaty, Ph.D
Pastor, Long Hollow Baptist Church
Author, *Growing Up* and *The Forgotten Jesus*

The unchanging Gospel of Jesus Christ is the hope of our ever changing world. But what if our presentation of it keeps people from hearing it or responding to it? That's the premise of Ken Ham's new book. The majority of our young people leave the church when they leave home and never return. Why? Because they were never taught how to defend their faith or how to deal with their doubts. What if we could change that? What if we could equip believers in every age and stage of life to boldly and effectively share the Good News and stand up for the truth of God's Word instead of standing down when the Bible is under attack? The church no longer has home field advantage in the world. But we can still win, and Ken Ham shows us how.

> Barry Cameron, Sr. Pastor
> Crossroads Christian, Grand Prairie, Texas

Things have changed, yes even the world we live in. However, our message is unchanging and Ken Ham gives clear, concise, and compelling hope to reach this changing world with the good news of Christ."

> Dr. Johnny Hunt
> Sr. Pastor, First Baptist Church Woodstock
> Past President of the Southern Baptist Convention

When we understand the times, we will know what to do. This even includes the way that we communicate the gospel with other people. The *Gospel Reset* book by Ken Ham presents the enormous challenges we face today, but thankfully, it also gives us practical ways we can communicate this gospel in a relevant way effectively. Anyone who desires to share Christ with other people or proclaim God's Word in today's world, needs to read this book. Get one for yourself and then share another one with a friend.

> Dr. Ronnie Floyd, Senior Pastor, Cross Church
> President, National Day of Prayer
> Past President, Southern Baptist Convention

My friend Ken Ham is stubborn for the truth. He is a bulldog for the gospel. When he gets his Aussie teeth into something, he won't let it go. His message is uncompromising, compassionate, encouraging, and most timely. Please, read this book and pass it on to those you love.

> Ray Comfort, Evangelist & CEO, Living Waters

Gospel Reset

salvation made
RELEVANT

KEN HAM

First printing: April 2018
Third printing: August 2018

Master Books®, P.O. Box 726, Green Forest, AR 72638
Master Books® is a division of the New Leaf Publishing Group, Inc.

ISBN: 978-1-68344-114-4
ISBN: 978-1-61458-657-9 (digital)
Library of Congress Number: 2018936319

Cover by Diana Bogardus

Please consider requesting that a copy of this volume be purchased by your local library system.

Printed in the United States of America

Please visit our website for other great titles:
www.masterbooks.com

For information regarding author interviews,
please contact the publicity department at (870) 438-5288.

Master
Books®
A Division of New Leaf Publishing Group
www.masterbooks.com

Dedication

To my godly mother, who at the time of the writing of this book celebrated her 90th birthday. Her boldness in sharing Christ with others, prayers, godly wisdom, uncompromising stand on God's Word, and dedication to her family have left a legacy to her children, grandchildren, and great-grandchildren that will continue to impact millions with the saving gospel message.

Contents

Note from the Author

Billy Graham passed away February 21, 2018. Many news items reported on his death and paid tribute to this great evangelist. One headline[1] really stood out to me:

> **There will never be another Billy Graham, because the world that made him possible is gone**

This was similar to what Fox News political commentator Tucker Carlson stated during his short tribute to Billy Graham on *Tucker Carlson Tonight,* February 21, 2018:

> He basically just preached the Bible. In the America of the time that was enough.

---

1. https://www.yahoo.com/news/will-never-another-billy-graham-world-made-possible-gone-195847056.html.

People stopped him on the street to shake his hand. We live in a different country now, but Billy Graham never changed.

Yes, the world has changed, we do "live in a different country" now, and another Billy Graham would not have the same response as the late great Billy Graham the evangelist had.

The gospel message hasn't changed, but the way in which it needs to be presented in a secularized culture does need to change. The way to present the gospel does need to be reset in the world we now live in.

Foreword
Bodie Hodge

The Western World — from North America to Europe to Australia — has changed. It's not like it was in the days of Billy Graham, when thousands just stood and listened to the gospel (good news about Jesus) and responded. Evangelism in our culture today seems difficult and sometimes impossible. We preach Jesus, and people don't seem to care. Why?

Allow me to explain, but first, permit me to preface it by discussing Latin America. I was on a trip to Peru speaking in churches and conferences and seeing some sites. At one point, one of our guides was leading a group of us Bible-believing Christians to see a whale graveyard in the desert. It was a long bus ride.

Our guide had related that he was raised Catholic, but in speaking with him I saw that he was heavily influenced by the religion of secular humanism. For example, he professed "millions of years" and evolution.

As we ventured out to the site with the whale fossils, our guide mentioned that these fossils were millions of years old. Our group kindly disagreed with him and said that we followed the Bible. We believed the majority of fossils, including the whale fossils in question, were a result of the Flood of Noah's day.

He seemed intrigued and he asked us to clarify. We told him that the rock layers that the whales were in couldn't be both millions of years old and at the same time buried in the Flood sediment. We further elaborated that the rock layers were either formed in the Flood or were laid down slowly over millions of years (with no major catastrophes as the secularists teach).

Our guide paused for a moment in thought. Then he said, "Hmmm. God can't be wrong, so the idea of millions of years in the fossil record have to be wrong." He was incredibly relieved to know that he didn't have to believe in long ages and evolution anymore. It was like a switch just turned on for him and it all made sense. I was actually shocked and unprepared for his response. I turned to the gents with me, who were fellow Christians who believe the Genesis account, and said, "Well, that was easy."

I realized that he was raised to believe a global Flood in his Catholic education, but at the same time, he was taught millions of years and evolution. When this issue finally came to a head, he had enough of a foundation to realize that the Bible was true regarding the Flood.

Bring this back to our Western Culture. I don't get responses like this. I get people who are so engrained with big bang, millions of years, and evolution, that those are "untouchable" in their worldview — sadly, this is even the case within many churches, Christian colleges, and seminaries, too.

But the problem is worse than you may think. I've told people about Jesus and I get responses like, "Jesus who?" I've told people that Jesus is the Son of God and I get responses like, "Which god are you talking about — Zeus, Thor, Allah, or some other one?" I've pointed out that people are sinners and need to be saved from their sin, and I've had people say, "What is sin?"

I realized that we are in a culture that has indeed changed. They no longer have the foundational information about God, His Word, and their need for salvation. Our culture, and even many within the Church, have such a minute understanding of Scripture, particularly the early pages of Genesis, that they have little to no foundation to understand the message of Jesus. Unlike the foundation of our guide in Peru, many in our culture simply don't have *any* foundation to comprehend the message of Christ, ever since the Bible and Christianity have been kicked out of schools and replaced with the godless religion of secular humanism.

The sad part is that churches are largely doing business as usual, telling people about Jesus without the foundational knowledge for Christ. It isn't working like it used to in the West.

But God didn't leave us in the dark. A careful analysis of Scripture and early missions work by the Apostles Peter and Paul reveal the answer. Ken Ham dives into this subject brilliantly to teach churches and Christians how to evangelize and preach Christ in our culture today. What we need, to share the truth of God's Word and Gospel of Jesus Christ in our changed Western World, is a gospel reset.

INTRODUCTION

Something is happening to America — in fact, to the entire once-Christianized Western world. Whether you get your news from television or online, the information is the same. The United States is no longer the country she once was. It is shocking to compare the worldview of today's generation with the one embraced by older generations in the West.

America has the largest number of Christian churches, colleges, seminaries, resources, and media of any nation in the world. Yet, her values and predominant worldview demonstrate that America is becoming less Christian every day. Western culture is changing. In fact, Western civilization as a whole is becoming less Christian in its worldview, whether it's the United Kingdom, Europe, or Australia. We are seeing moral relativism spread throughout Western

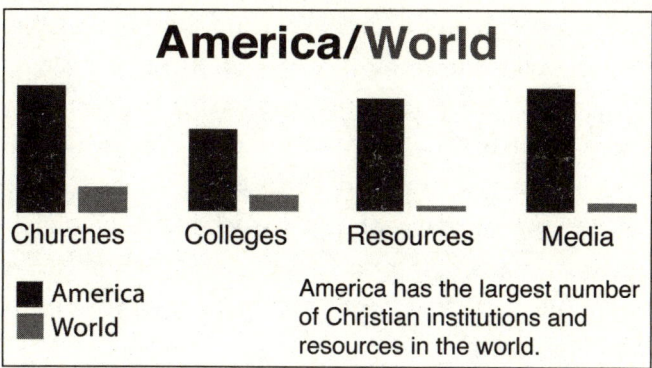

America/World

Churches Colleges Resources Media

■ America
■ World

America has the largest number of Christian institutions and resources in the world.

culture like an infectious disease. There's even talk that an ideological civil war is being waged in America. And as moral relativism enjoys greater national acceptance, Christians and their worldview are treated with increasing intolerance.

The elimination of prayer and the Bible from state schools was only the beginning. Now Christians themselves are being targeted for the free exercise of their faith in the public sphere. Nativity scenes, Ten Commandments, and crosses have been systematically and progressively removed from public places.

Even terminology associated with Christian teaching is being changed or removed. For example, "Merry Christmas" is changed to "Happy Holidays." In short, Christianity's influence is slowly being purged from America's national conscience.

Simultaneously, Christians are not having an impact on culture and those in it, choosing instead to remain content and safe within their own churches and Christian circles. We are not imparting the gospel in a way the next generation can grasp. Of course, the message of the gospel hasn't changed, but the way people *think* has changed dramatically. Therefore, we must speak the truth of Scripture in the language of culture.

What we're seeing is a "divide" in the West. First, I would like to explain and define this divide. Then I will relate it to preaching the gospel and how the Church can influence the culture through being salt and light. I see this as a critical moment in Church history, for if churches don't wake up, recognize this divide, and make the necessary "gospel reset," particularly regarding the Millennial generation, then we are going to lose the next generation and effectively destroy the Church's influence in our country.

There's no doubt there is a widening chasm between the older generation and the Millennials in America. The older generation, even those who aren't Christian, have more of a Christianized worldview because of the significant past influence of Christianity. Today's younger generations do not have such a worldview because their thinking has been secularized through education and culture. This, then, is the divide we're seeing. Understanding the difference between these worldviews is an essential first step to having an impact on this generation with the gospel.

In Acts 2, Peter preached to Jews, while in Acts 17, Paul preached to Greeks. Their approaches were different based upon the worldviews of their audiences. The Jews in Acts 2 believed, thought, and viewed their world from a Jewish perspective. They already knew and understood what the Bible teaches about creation, sin, and other topics. However, the Greeks in Acts 17 did not have a foundational knowledge of biblical teachings on creation, sin, or other matters.

America, as a culture (in fact, the entire Western world), used to be like "Jews" in this respect. But that's no longer the case. Our culture has declined, having become more like the "Greeks." Biblical illiteracy (i.e., having little or no knowledge about God and the Bible) is becoming the rule rather than the exception. Even so, most churches still teach kids in their Sunday schools as if we are still in this "Jewish" style culture, instead of the "Greek" culture we find ourselves in. And why don't more churches recognize this? Because the Church has actually contributed to this lack of understanding. More about this later.

Through this book, I trust your eyes will be opened to gain an understanding of why this great divide is happening in our Western countries. For Christians, the more we understand the nature of this divide in our nation, the better we can understand how to close the gap and respond to what's happening, hopefully before it's too late. And if we do, I believe it will open a door, enabling us to powerfully impact and influence this present-day "Greek" culture with the gospel.

MILLENNIAL "LINGO"

Did you know that Millennials speak a different language? (Millennials are considered those born between approximately 1982 and 2002.)

For example, generations ago, when one said the word *God* in the public schools (government schools), most kids and teachers thought of the Creator-God of the Bible. But today, if you say the word *God* in the public schools, most students and teachers would respond, "Which *god* are you referring to? The Muslim god? A Hindu god? The Buddhist concept of god? Or a New Age god?"

In previous generations, when you said in Sunday school, "Let's read a Bible story," most kids anticipated hearing something that happened in history from the Bible. (By the way, the word *story* is taken from the Latin word *historia*,[1] which commonly meant just that — *history*.)

However, when you say "Bible *story*" today, most kids (and adults) think "fiction" or "fairy tale." That is because of this "divide" in generational thinking. Many do not see the Bible as authoritative, trustworthy, infallible, or inerrant, largely because they have been indoctrinated by secular culture and education. So, they simply dismiss Scripture as a "fairy tale."

To further illustrate these generational differences, consider how the same words can have very different meanings, depending on who is listening.

When my wife and I first came over to America from my native country of Australia in 1987, I would tell people we came over as missionaries to a "pagan" culture. Of course, people would laugh because America had such dominant Christian influence, much more than Australia.

But, sadly, when we look at America today, this has become a reality. From a worldview perspective, America has become much more pagan. I thought it would be easy living in a country like America because we spoke the same language — English. At least I didn't have to learn another language! But I

---

1. *Merriam-Webster*, s.v. "Story," under "Origin and Etymology of Story," accessed January 4, 2018, https://www.merriam-webster.com/dictionary/story.

was so wrong! I found Americans didn't speak English after all — at least not the same English I spoke. I speak Australian-English, while Americans speak American-English, which is a different (English) language altogether.

Yet even though you may speak the same basic language, it is still important that you define the meanings of certain words. Otherwise, you won't be able to communicate very well.

After moving to California, I had a problem with my car. So, I asked someone, "Hey, can you help me? My battery is flat."

"Your battery is what?" he replied.

"Flat," I said.

"Did you run over it?" he responded.

I said, "No, I left the lights on."

He then exclaimed, "Oh, you mean your battery is dead!"

"Dead?" I said. "It wasn't ever alive in the first place! How can the thing die if it wasn't alive!"

Another time I asked someone where I could find the nearest petrol station. They had no idea what I was talking about. I said, "I need to put the stuff in my car that makes it go."

"Oh, you need a gas station!" she replied.

"Gas?" I thought. "You don't put gas in your car. You put liquid in there!"

So, Americans call "gas" what we call "petrol" in Australia.

But by far my most embarrassing experience occurred when I told someone on the telephone that I was "nursing our baby." I couldn't figure out why there was a long silence on the phone! After some research I found out that nursing a baby in America has a very different meaning to what it does in Australia. In Australia, nursing a baby means holding a baby, but in America, nursing a baby means breast-feeding a baby. How embarrassing to think that people in America thought I was telling them I was breast-feeding our baby!

It didn't take me long to realize there was a lot I had to learn about American English.

Here's the point: I recognized, even coming from another English-speaking country, that if you don't understand how words are used in a particular context, you will have a serious communication problem. The divide between the older generations and the younger generations in our Western world has led to an even greater communication problem than this. Just like with the word *God*, there are many words today that no longer mean what they used to.

If we fail to understand these sorts of changes, we won't understand this great divide that's occurring in our culture. Worse, we won't understand how to effectively communicate the gospel to the younger generations.

MILLENNIALS
AND THE CHURCH

When we had America's Research Group conduct the research on the Ark project to find out how many people would visit a full-size Ark in 2016, the research indicated we would see 1.4 to 2.2 million visitors per year.

As part of this research project, we also had our researchers ask questions about the spiritual state of this nation. In this general population study, they asked, "If you attended church regularly as a child, do you still attend most Sundays or did you stop attending?" In research conducted in 2015, we found that 22% of people in their sixties who used to go to church have stopped attending. But with the Millennial generation, that number was over half (53%).

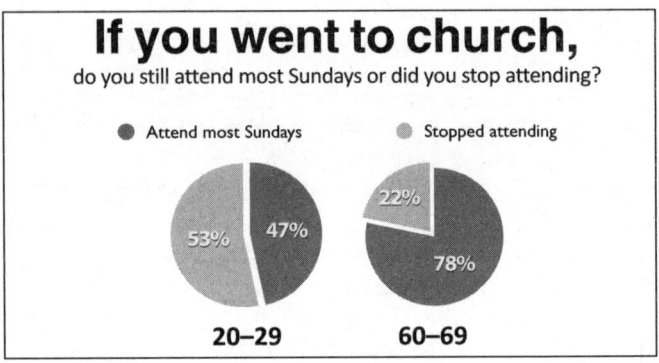

If you went to church,
do you still attend most Sundays or did you stop attending?

● Attend most Sundays　　　● Stopped attending

53%　47%

22%

78%

20–29　　　　　　**60–69**

Answers in Genesis also contracted with America's Research Group to conduct focused research on these American Millennials who have now left the Church. Statistics revealed that two-thirds of young people are leaving the Church in America by the time they reach college age, and very few are returning. If that exodus trend continues, we'll end up like England, where only about 4–5% of the total population are attending church. At the conclusion of this research, we wrote the book *Already Gone*, detailing the results and our observations.

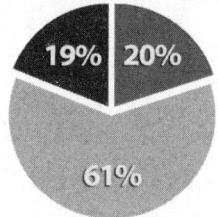

Twentysomethings
struggle to stay active in Christian faith

19%   20%

61%

● 20% Churched as teen, spiritually active at age 29
● 61% Churched as teen, disengaged during twenties
● 19% Never churched as teen, still unconnected

In 2015, AiG also had America's Research Group conduct research on those Millennials who still regularly attend church in America. This was quite an extensive research project, and the results were published in a book called *Ready to Return*. The title doesn't mean these Millennials should be ready to return to church, since they already attend church, but rather that they needed to return to the authority of God's Word.

Here is just a glimpse at some of the research results. When asked, "Do you consider yourself 'born again'?" — 40% of Millennials who attend church outright said "no."

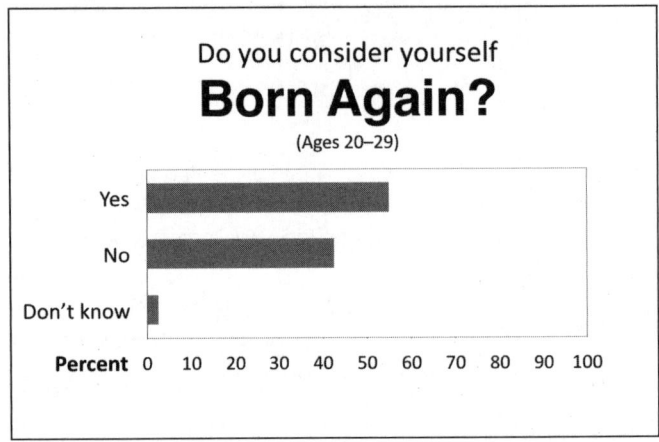

"Do you believe if you're a good person you will get to heaven?" — 65% of these church-going Millennials outright said "yes." This means the 40% figure for those who say they are not "born again" is actually too low! Obviously, many don't understand what being born again really means.

"Should gay couples be allowed to marry?" — 40% outright said "yes" and 10% said "don't know," which means that 50% of these Millennials who regularly attend church do not oppose gay "marriage."

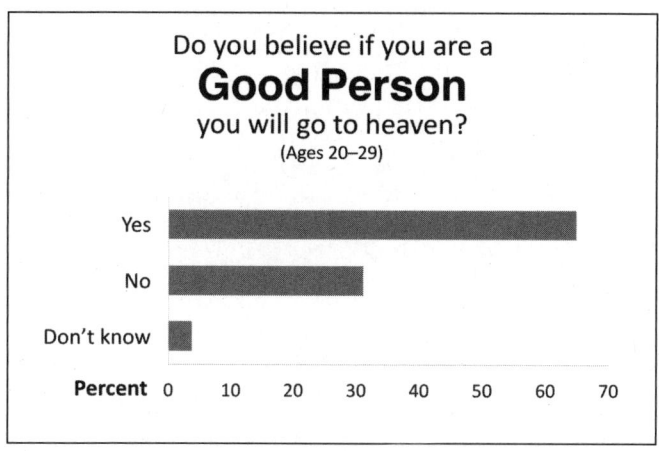

These statistics reveal that something tragic is happening to coming generations, and it's having drastic consequences on the Church right now and her influence on culture.

WHY IS THIS
HAPPENING?

I believe (and the research in various ways confirmed) one of the biggest reasons so many Millennials are leaving the Church, and why the ones who remain are confused, is that we haven't shown them how to defend their faith. We haven't taught them answers to skeptical questions that cause them to doubt and disbelieve the Scriptures. We haven't taught them apologetics. We've given them answers to some of the "what?" but not nearly enough of the "why?"

At Answers in Genesis, the Creation Museum, and the Ark Encounter, we specialize in teaching apologetics by equipping people for how to answer today's skeptical questions that cause many to doubt the Bible. Sadly, most of our churches, pastors, Sunday school teachers, seminary professors, Bible

college professors, and Christian college professors are instructing coming generations that they don't need to believe in a literal Genesis. Instead, they're propagating the lie that a Christian can believe in evolution and its millions of years. By and large, most of these young people have been told that it doesn't really matter how they view Genesis, and that it's not important anyway. But it is. How you view Genesis dictates how you see and interpret the rest of the Bible. If Genesis cannot be trusted to be an accurate account of mankind's beginnings and the origin of sin and God's provision of salvation, then how can we trust it or any other books of the Bible when they make truth claims?

Today, 90–95% of kids from church homes attend public schools, where they are taught that

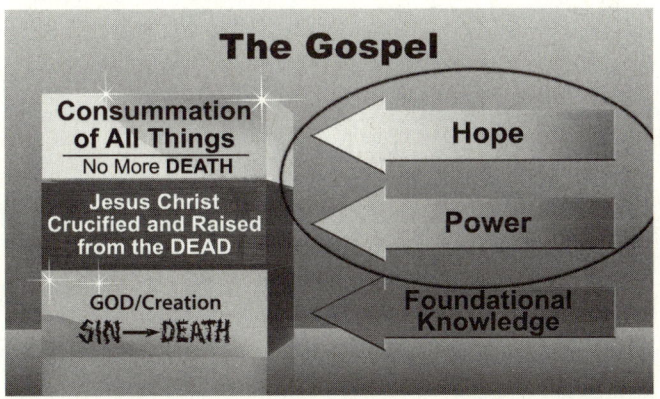

evolution (biological, geological, astronomical, anthropological) is fact and not the unsupportable belief that it is. In these schools, the Bible has been ignored and ridiculed. Scripture's God is mocked, taught as myth, or even relegated to a banned topic. These schools have essentially replaced Christianity with their religion of secularism, as students are taught that life and the universe are explained by natural processes, apart from the supernatural intervention of a Creator. Students are indoctrinated with what is called "scientific evidence" that supposedly disproves the Bible's account of origins. Sadly, most Christian parents and Church leaders haven't taught these students how to defend the Christian faith against such secular attacks. Most churches and Christian homes have not equipped young people with answers to the skeptical questions and statements they hear concerning the Bible. The result of this is that many of them begin privately doubting God's Word by middle school age, eventually walking away from the Christian church.

BUILDING A PROPER/SOLID FOUNDATION

If you ask the average churchgoing Christian today, "Considering what's happening in the culture, what do we need to do?" most will respond, "Well, we just need to go out and proclaim the gospel." But exactly what do they mean by "the gospel"? Many Christians today fail to fully understand the gospel, and therefore are unable to share it effectively. I believe this is due to a foundational problem.

Let me explain. Imagine buying an Agatha Christie murder mystery book. Would you flip to the end, find out "who done it," and then throw the book away? Of course not. No one does this because in order to understand the end of the story, you must first understand the plot that is found in the rest of the book. But that's essentially what's happening today with the way people in the Church read the Bible. Most tend to start toward the end of the book, so they don't understand the plot.

We have generations who don't understand the Bible's original plot — the beginning. Therefore, they don't fully understand the subsequent message of Jesus dying on the Cross and being raised from the dead. They also don't understand why they need to believe in Christ in order to be saved.

When I ask people in the Church, "What is the gospel?" I hear people say, "Well, it's the good news: Jesus died on the Cross and was raised from the dead."

And while this is true, you can't really understand the good news of the gospel unless you first understand the bad news found in Genesis. Many in the

Church say we need to go out and "get people saved." But consider this — most people don't yet even know they're lost! So, why would they believe they need to be saved? Saved from what? Saved by whom? Saved for what purpose? You see, unless people realize their need for a Savior, telling them that Jesus "loves them" means very little.

Some of today's research has revealed that a large percentage of our population does believe they're "sinners," but only a small percentage believe that Jesus Christ enables them to overcome sin. But to be honest, most don't even know what sin actually is. Even within our churches, many Christians can't accurately define what sin really means.

I used to be a teacher, and I come from a long line of teachers, including my father, grandfather, and great-grandfather. I jokingly tell people that my teaching heritage goes back "millions of years!" But one of the things I always tried to do as a teacher was to communicate in such a way that my students would understand. That's because I wanted them to "get it."

I would present information logically as if I were building a house. And how do you normally build a house? Do you start with the roof, and then build the walls, after which you construct the foundation? Of

Start with the foundation, build the walls,
and then the roof.

course not! When building a house, a builder always
begins with the foundation, and then the walls, and
then the roof.

Explaining the gospel works the same way. We
first start with the foundational teaching that God is
Creator, and that sin and death entered the world, as
recorded in Genesis. That's the foundational knowledge needed to understand the next part — the
"walls" — that God sent His Son to die on the Cross
and be raised from the dead, because death is the penalty for sin. This is the power of the gospel, and why
Christ can offer us the free gift of salvation. Then we
put on the "roof." One day there's going to be a new

heaven and a new earth. So, there we have the gospel, beginning with Genesis and ending with Revelation. It's really like building a house from the foundation to the roof.

I contend that many people in our churches today try to build Christian doctrines into their kids (or when witnessing to others) by starting with the roof, then the walls, without even considering building the foundation.

But we must always begin with the foundation before building the walls and the roof. It sounds so logical and basic, but it seems many Christians don't understand this when it comes to the Christian worldview.

Here's another problem: When witnessing to a non-Christian and dealing with issues like gay "marriage," abortion, or racism, what we tend to do is try to impose the "walls" and "roof" on them, when they don't yet have the correct foundation for that structure. Until they understand the foundation for the Christian worldview, we won't be able to communicate to them in a way that will put them on the right road to understanding the gospel.

Many Christians are guilty of only preaching part of the gospel, specifically the power and hope of the gospel. But when you preach the power and the hope of the gospel, you're assuming the foundation has already been laid. This is a faulty assumption, especially in our post-Christian, godless culture. In this current moral climate, we can never assume that people possess a foundational knowledge concerning creation, sin, and death. When you hear preachers talk about the gospel, you mostly hear the "walls" and "roof" of the gospel. You will hear them preach that Jesus died on the Cross for your sin and was raised from the dead. People will be challenged to put their faith and trust in the Lord Jesus Christ. But do the generations we are preaching to today really understand what sin is, why there is death in the world, and who Jesus is? I don't think so. It's like being told by a doctor that you need an operation, but he has yet to reveal what's wrong with you or why you need it! In generations past, most had a basic understanding of sin and their sinful condition before God. But this is no longer true for upcoming younger generations.

PETER'S
SERMON

In today's culture, we have generations who are products of a very secular education system that has, by and large, eliminated the Bible and God from their education experience. And in the Church, we have ignored or compromised the Genesis account. As a result, many young people attending church today have not been taught the foundational history necessary to truly understand the gospel. Further, young people in our culture don't understand what the word *sin* means. They don't understand who Jesus really is or comprehend what it means to say they're a sinner. They have no clue as to why our world has so much death and suffering.

To illustrate the difference between previous and present generations, let's consider two sermons given in Scripture. The first is found in Acts 2, where Peter preaches the gospel to the Jews (or those already familiar with the Old Testament religion). In generations past, Western culture was much like Jewish culture in this respect. They were acquainted with the fundamental truths of Scripture.

Look at the sermon Peter preached in Acts 2:14–36:

> But Peter, standing with the eleven, lifted up his voice and addressed them: "Men of Judea and all who dwell in Jerusalem, let this be known to you, and give ear to my words. For these people are not drunk, as you suppose, since it is only the third hour of the day. But this is what was uttered through the prophet Joel:
>
> > "And in the last days it shall be, God declares, that I will pour out my Spirit on all flesh, and your sons and your daughters shall prophesy, and your young men shall see visions, and your old men shall dream dreams; even on my male servants and female servants in those days I will pour out my Spirit, and they shall prophesy.

And I will show wonders in the heavens above and signs on the earth below, blood, and fire, and vapor of smoke; the sun shall be turned to darkness and the moon to blood, before the day of the Lord comes, the great and magnificent day. And it shall come to pass that everyone who calls upon the name of the Lord shall be saved."

"Men of Israel, hear these words: Jesus of Nazareth, a man attested to you by God with mighty works and wonders and signs that God did through him in your midst, as you yourselves know — this Jesus, delivered up according to the definite plan and foreknowledge of God, you crucified and killed by the hands of lawless men. God raised him up, loosing the pangs of death, because it was not possible for him to be held by it. For David says concerning him,

"I saw the Lord always before me, for he is at my right hand that I may not be shaken; therefore my heart was glad, and my tongue rejoiced; my flesh also will dwell in hope. For you will not abandon my soul to Hades, or let your Holy One see corruption. You have made known to me the paths of life; you will make me full of gladness with your presence.

"Brothers, I may say to you with confidence about the patriarch David that he both died and was buried, and his tomb is with us to this day. Being therefore a prophet, and knowing that God had sworn with an oath to him that he would set one of his descendants on his throne, he foresaw and spoke about the resurrection of the Christ, that he was not abandoned to Hades, nor did his flesh see corruption. This Jesus God raised up, and of that we all are witnesses. Being therefore exalted at the right hand of God, and having received from the Father the promise of the Holy Spirit, he has poured out this that you yourselves are seeing and hearing. For David did not ascend into the heavens, but he himself says,

> "The Lord said to my Lord, 'Sit at my right hand, until I make your enemies your footstool.' "

Let all the house of Israel therefore know for certain that God has made him both Lord and Christ, this Jesus whom you crucified."

You can imagine Peter standing on the Temple steps on the day of Pentecost as he preached this very bold message. People were probably bringing their sacrifices as Peter preached:

"… this Jesus, delivered up according to the definite plan and foreknowledge of God, you crucified and killed by the hands of lawless men. God raised him up, loosing the pangs of death, because it was not possible for him to be held by it" (Acts 2:23–24).

So, after hearing this sermon, how did they respond?

Now when they heard this they were cut to the heart, and said to Peter and the rest of the apostles, "Brothers, what shall we do?" And Peter said to them, "Repent and be baptized every one of you in the name of Jesus Christ for the forgiveness of your sins, and you will receive the gift of the Holy Spirit. For the promise is for you and for your children and for all who are far off, everyone whom the Lord our God calls to himself."

> And with many other words he bore witness
> and continued to exhort them, saying, "Save
> yourselves from this crooked generation." So
> those who received his word were baptized,
> and there were added that day about three
> thousand souls (Acts 2:37–41).

Wow! Wouldn't you like to see a revival like that in our day? We used to see crusades like that in America, but we're certainly not seeing them now. We also once experienced them in the United Kingdom, but we're not seeing such revivals now. We've even seen crusades greatly influence Australia, but we haven't seen such happening in a long time. Why don't we see more gatherings where thousands of people basically fall on their knees before the Holy God, repent of their sin, be saved, and go on to influence the culture with the Christian message? What we have to ask ourselves is, "Why did this happen then, in Acts 2, but not in America today?" Obviously, this began the explosion of the Church's growth and thus a launching point for the gospel in the Christian era. However, we still don't see this type of phenomenon today. Why not?

First, let's consider Peter's audience. Who was he preaching to? Primarily Jews or those already convinced of, or familiar with, the Jewish religion. This scenario sets that stage for us to understand what happened here and why. At this point in their history, did Peter's audience believe in God? Yes, they did.

When Peter said the word *God*, who did they think of? It would have been the one God, the Creator God of Genesis. Did they know what was meant by the term *sin*? Absolutely! They knew about Adam and Eve and the Fall of man. They understood they were sinners. And did they know why death was in the world? Of course. They understood that death originated because of sin. They knew about the blood sacrifice as a covering for their sin as recorded in Genesis 3:21. They were at the Temple sacrificing animals *because* of sin. They understood the need for a blood sacrifice because of their sin in Adam. (The Bible teaches that Adam was the head of the human race. We are all descendants of Adam; what he did we did also, because he represented each of us — and we all come from Adam, the first man.)

They were aware of the promise of a Messiah given in Genesis 3:15. The point is that they possessed the foundational knowledge necessary to understand the message of salvation. Therefore, Peter could safely assume that when he used biblical terminology, his audience would understand the meaning the same way he did. They knew about the one Creator God, sin, and why death was in the world. They knew about

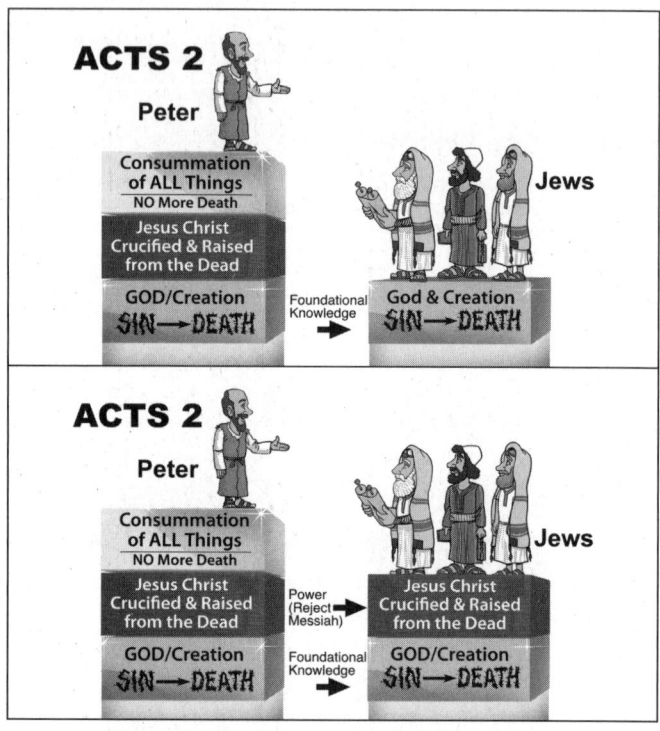

the promise of a Savior. They had the history in Genesis concerning Adam and Eve and the Fall of man embedded into their national conscience. And they knew the first blood sacrifice in Genesis was a covering for their sin.

They would have been very familiar with the promise of a Savior in Genesis 3:15:

> "I will put enmity between you and the woman, and between your offspring and her offspring; he shall bruise your head, and you shall bruise his heel."

Then in Genesis 3:21, Moses tells us about the first blood sacrifice as a covering for Adam and Eve's sin, when God provided coats of skins to them (the origin of clothing):

> And the LORD God made for Adam and for his wife garments of skins and clothed them.

So, the Jews had the foundational knowledge needed to understand the gospel. Peter didn't have to work to convince them God's Word was true. He didn't have to try to convince them that there is one Creator God. He didn't have to define sin. Nor did he have to convince them that there was such a thing as sin. Peter could assume he was in a creation-based culture and those he was speaking to understood the terms he was using. No "pre-evangelism" was needed.

Now in reality, there are actually only two religions in the world. The origin of these two religions begins in Genesis 2 and 3. In Genesis 2, God told Adam to obey him and not eat the fruit of one specific tree. Adam was told to obey God's Word.

The Lord God took the man and put him in the garden of Eden to work it and keep it. And the Lord God commanded the man, saying, 'You may surely eat of every tree of the garden, but of the tree of the knowledge of good and evil you shall not eat, for in the day that you eat of it you shall surely die' (Genesis 2:15–17).

However, in Genesis 3, the devil comes (using a serpent) and tempts Eve:

Now the serpent was more crafty than any other beast of the field that the Lord God had made.

He said to the woman, "Did God actually say, 'You shall not eat of any tree in the garden'?" And the woman said to the serpent, "We may eat of the fruit of the trees in the garden, but God said, 'You shall not eat of the fruit of the tree that is in the midst of the garden, neither shall you touch it, lest you die.'" But the serpent said to the woman, "You will not surely die. For God knows that when you eat of it your eyes will be opened, and you will be like God, knowing good and evil" (Genesis 3:1–5).

These passages tell us of a great divide — a divide between God's Word and man's word (the temptation for man to be his own god — "you will be like God"). It's a divide between two religions, two worldviews, two starting points. Simply put, there are only two ways to build your thinking. You can start with the One who knows everything, who has always been there, and who has revealed to us what we need to know. Beginning with Him, we can build a solid and accurate worldview based on God's Word. The only other starting point is with sinful man's fallible word. But by adding man's word to God's Word (e.g., adding evolution/millions of years to Genesis), you end up compromising God's Word, and your starting point is flawed from the beginning. It's no longer God's infallible truth. Your starting point then is man's inherently fallible word.

So, the Jews had the right beginning. They had the right history. They had the right starting point of God's Word (the writings of Moses, beginning in

Genesis). They were on the correct "road" and heading to an accurate understanding of the gospel. That "road," beginning with creation, the Fall of man, and the promise of the Seed and the Messiah (Genesis 3:15; Daniel 9:24–27; etc.), is the right foundation to understand the message of who Jesus is and why He died and rose from the dead. This "road" they were on led up to the message of the Cross, even though many Jews rejected the idea that Jesus is the Messiah. This truth became a real stumbling block to their understanding and acceptance of the saving gospel as presented in the New Testament. Paul stated:

> . . . but we preach Christ crucified, a stumbling block to Jews and folly to Gentiles (1 Corinthians 1:23).

JEWS/ACTS 2

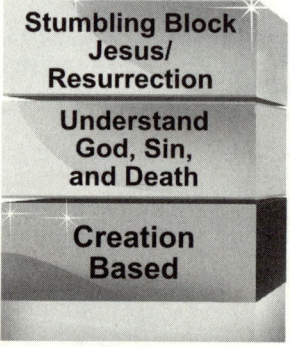

AN ACTS 2-TYPE CULTURE

As I mentioned before, I come from Australia. I know many Americans point to the fact that their Founding Fathers had great convictions concerning the truth of the Bible. I tell people that our founding fathers in Australia also had great convictions too — but convictions of a different sort! You see, Australia was founded as a convict settlement. Thus, Australia did not enjoy the foundational Christian influence in its history that America had. But Australia did inherit the British system of government, which was originally rooted in Christian thinking.

In 1959 and again in the 1960s, evangelist Billy Graham came to Australia, preaching several major crusades. His main message was this: You are sinners.

Sydney Showground as crowds begin arriving to hear
Billy Graham in Sydney, Australia on April 12, 1959.
The crowd would reach 150,000 between this and
an adjoining stadium that night. (SMH Picture by George
Lipman, courtesy of Fairfax Syndication)

You need to believe God's Word. You need to repent
of your sin and trust in Jesus as your Savior.

Through this simple yet powerful message, thousands of people were converted. It is said that this was
the closest Australia has ever come to revival. Most
people in Australia have never gone to church. Also,
apparently church attendance dropped off markedly

after World War I.[1] Actual numbers are difficult to ascertain because if someone claims they are "Christian" on the census, this doesn't necessarily mean they attend church regularly or are what would be defined as "born-again" Christians. Christian leaders in Australia whom I have spoken to believe regular church attendance is probably more like England's is today (5%),[2] making the number of truly born-again Christians quite small. This is very different from America. Australia has never had the Christianized foundation America has had. Many of America's Founding Fathers were Christian, or they at least respected the Christian faith and used parts of the Bible to frame their thinking.

But what's interesting about all this is that when Billy Graham preached at those Australian crusades, he didn't really define what sin was. He didn't give specific foundational teaching from Genesis or define what he meant by the word *God*. Instead, he basically assumed people would understand the terms he was using in the same way he did. And, by and large, I would say that was so. But do you know why?

---

1. Robert D. Linder, *The Long Tragedy: Australian Evangelical Christians and the Great War, 1914–1918* (Adelaide, South Australia: Openbook Publishers, 2000.)

2. Brierley Consultancy, "Christianity in the UK," *Faith Survey*, https://faithsurvey.co.uk/uk-christianity.html, accessed January 4, 2018.

Back in 1959, when I was a little boy in primary school (elementary school), it was mandatory for teachers in Australia to read through the Bible during the year (because Australia inherited the British educational system). Even when I went to high school in the 1960s, students recited the Lord's Prayer on parade (assembly) before we went to our classes for the day. Hardly any kids in my class or school went to church, but we nevertheless stood there repeating, "Our Father, which art in heaven, hallowed be thy name...." We recited the Lord's Prayer!

Australia used to be an Acts 2-type culture, even though the culture didn't have a real Christian foundation like America did. Even so, kids and adults understood terms like *God* and *sin*. When someone said "Adam and Eve," most Australians knew who Adam and Eve were. If one talked about the nativity, most understood the account of the babe in a manger. Most knew about Noah's Flood and the Bible's account of Jonah and the great fish. They also knew about Jesus raising people from the dead and healing the blind and the lame. Even though the majority didn't go to Sunday school, they knew about these accounts because the Bible was read and respected at school — *state schools*.

However, if an evangelist were to preach a similar message in Australia today using the same biblical terms Graham used, I don't believe we would see thousands converted as happened in the 1950s and '60s. And why not? What's the difference between now (21st century) and the mid-20th century in Australia?

Australia (like the rest of the West) is no longer an Acts 2-type culture. The Western culture has undergone a dramatic change. America is also losing its Acts 2 culture. In America, God, the Bible, and prayer have all but been eliminated from public (state-run) schools. Evolution is now taught as fact, not as the unfounded idea that it is. Public schools are extremely secular, teaching generations of students the religion of naturalism (atheism). We now have increasing numbers of students who have come through the education system but have never gone to church, and they have virtually no teaching from the Bible. Of course, it isn't the government's job to equip young people with the Scriptures. That task is the responsibility of parents and the Church. However, God does expect governments to acknowledge Him as Creator and moral lawgiver.

Many today have no concept of the meaning of Christian terms. It is fundamentally a very different culture compared to that of generations past. We're seeing the great divide as this change is occurring before our very eyes. It really is sort of a "civil war," dividing the country between the Acts 2-type people and the Acts 17-type people, whom we'll discuss in the next section.

PAUL'S SERMON /
A CHRISTIAN ON "MARS"

In contrast to Peter's sermon to Jews in Acts 2, in Acts 17, Paul preaches the Gospel to the Greeks. Paul went to Mars Hill, in Athens, to the Greeks who were very religious. There were atheists and pantheists (both pantheism and atheism are religious philosophies). In Athens, there were idols, temples, and altars of all sorts. When Paul arrived there, he met the Epicureans, who were similar to what we would call atheists, and also the Stoics, who were like pantheists. There were others there as well. He preached to them the message of Jesus and the Resurrection — a similar message to the one Peter preached in Acts 2.

But notice their response. "What's this babbler saying?"

And also some of the Epicurean and Stoic philosophers were conversing with him. Some were saying, "What would this idle babbler wish to say?" Others said, "He seems to be a proclaimer of strange deities," — because he was preaching Jesus and the resurrection (Acts 17:18).

Paul's message was foolishness to them! He preached an Acts 2-type message, but the response was very different from those who responded to Peter. Paul would later write that the preaching of the Cross was a stumbling block to the Jews but foolishness to the Greeks (1 Corinthians 1:23). But exactly why was it foolishness to the Greeks? Because Greeks had no concept of a Creator God (one God) as the Jews did. They didn't have the history about Adam and Eve or the Fall of man in the Garden and the entrance of sin and death. They did not understand the sacrificial system God instituted in Genesis 3:21 (the first blood sacrifice as a covering for their sin, a picture of what was to come in Jesus Christ, the lamb of God who takes away the sin of the world). They had the wrong foundation, and because of this, they didn't understand the message of the Cross. Therefore, it was foolishness to them.

Many Greeks held to an evolution-based culture. They believed in a form of naturalism and opposed their fellow Greeks who were polytheistic. Darwin did not invent the concept of evolution — he just re-popularized a particular view of it with a supposed "scientific" justification. Whenever we see people rejecting the Creator God of Scripture, there is usually some evolutionary view substituted in an attempt to explain origins, life, and the universe. Many ancient Greeks were no different.

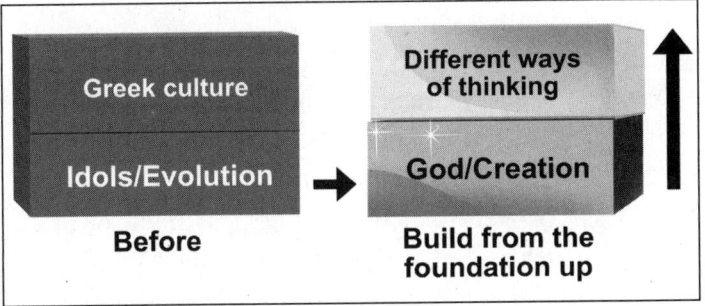

It's important to understand that Darwinian evolution is a religion.

Almost all atheistic evolutionists claim that because (supposedly) there is no God, their own worldview is not a religion. Many of them would argue that they have a "nonbelief."

One of the definitions of *religion* in the *Merriam-Webster Dictionary*, however, is this: "a cause, principle, or system of beliefs held to with ardor and faith."[1]

Atheism certainly fits that definition, and many of its adherents are quite zealous about their faith system.

Atheists have an active belief system with views concerning origins (molecules to man evolution — that the universe and life arose by natural processes): no life after death; denies the existence of God; how to behave while alive; and so much more. Honest atheists will admit their worldview is a faith. Atheistic evolution is a religion!

One candid atheist wrote, "My attitude is not based on science, but rather on faith. . . . The absence of a Creator, the non-existence of God is my childhood faith, my adult belief, unshakable and holy."[2]

Dr. Michael Ruse, from the Department of Philosophy at the University of Guelph in Ontario, is a philosopher of science, particularly of the evolutionary sciences. He is the author of several books on Darwinism and evolutionary ideas, and in an article in the *National Post*, he wrote:

---

1. *Merriam-Webster*, s.v. "Religion," accessed February 7, 2018, https://www.merriam-webster.com/dictionary/religion.
2. George Klein, *The Atheist in the Holy City* (Cambridge, MA: MIT Press, 1990), p. 203.

Evolution is promoted by its practitioners as more than mere science. Evolution is promulgated as an ideology, a secular religion — a full-fledged alternative to Christianity, with meaning and morality. . . . Evolution is a religion. This was true of evolution in the beginning, and it is true of evolution still today.[3]

The belief in millions of years is a part of the evolution religion built on naturalism (atheism), or the attempt to explain life without God. Sadly, much of the Church today in the 21st century has adopted this false religion of the age and simply added it into God's Word in Genesis. But is this any different from what we read about in the Bible's prophetic books? The Israelites adopted the false religions of surrounding nations and often added their own beliefs to the Jewish faith. By doing this, they compromised God's Word. And what happened to them? It destroyed their culture. And God judged them.

Because the Greeks were an evolution-based culture that had no understanding of biblical truth or terms like *God, sin*, etc., the message of the gospel was foolishness to them. But this highlights a very

---

3. Michael Ruse, "Saving Darwinism from the Darwinians," *National Post*, May 13, 2000, p. B-3.

important point. Peter preached the message of Jesus and the Cross in Acts 2, and the Jewish culture he spoke to, by and large, already had the foundation (understanding of a Creator God, the first man, the Fall, etc.), so he could build the "walls and the roof" (the message of the power of the gospel). However, when Paul preached the same basic message to the Greeks, the "walls and the roof" couldn't be built because the "structure" (worldview) didn't have the proper, pre-existing foundation.

AN ACTS 17-TYPE
CULTURE

We have a major problem in our Church and culture as a whole today because we have become like the Greeks. The majority of our Christian leaders have taught generations of kids and adults to believe in the evolution of life and man and/or millions of years. One of the most-asked questions by Millennials today goes something like this: "How can you believe in a loving God when there is so much death and suffering in the world?" They're perplexed when Christians talk about a loving God, as they see so many ugly things in this world — whether it's a devastating hurricane, earthquake, tidal wave, or mass shooting like the one in Las Vegas in October 2017.

Atheists regularly post on my social media platforms, making statements like, "Your God is a genocidal God, because look at all the death and suffering in the world. What about all the children starving and all these sicknesses? Where was your God when all those people were killed in Las Vegas? How can you say there's a loving God?"

But if they knew the holy, just God of the Bible, these things would be explained for them. The suffering and death we experience here are a result of man's sin, not God's cruelty. Senseless murders in our society can be traced back to Adam's disobedience and the depravity of the sin nature, not to God. Even sickness, disease, and injustice are all a result of sin entering the world. And this same God that atheists argue against (and that, ironically, they don't believe exists!) will one day right all wrongs and put an end to injustice, suffering, sin, and death. That's far more than the atheist evolutionist has to offer!

Now most kids go to public (state-run) schools. Even though there are some Christian teachers as missionaries in that education system, overall, the state education system has become very "Greek." For the most part, the Bible, prayer, and teaching of creation have been eliminated from this system. Evolutionary naturalism is now taught as *fact*. Atheism has become the state religion imposed on generations of kids. Overall, state schools have really become, in most instances (and increasingly so), "churches" of atheism. Educators indoctrinate their kids in a very secularized worldview. Most students today have little or no understanding of the history concerning the foundation of the West or the effect of the Reformation on Western culture.

What's happening in America, the United Kingdom, Australia, and in the whole Western world is that it's becoming more like the Greeks every day. Most kids are sent to the "Greek" education system, and they are turned into "Greeks." They have the wrong starting point (naturalism/evolution), and are, therefore, on the wrong road. And we wonder why they don't understand or accept the gospel. Christians are preaching to these generations as if they are "Jews," with messages like, "Repent of your sin and trust in Jesus." But to most, this message is foolishness and they simply don't understand it.

In my opinion, Christians also have a problem. Around 90–95 percent of kids from church homes go to the "Greek" education system, and they are also turned into "Greeks." They use the "Greek" Internet and watch the "Greek" television and read "Greek" books and magazines. They may be in our Sunday schools. And we may be preaching to them and teaching them about Jesus on the Cross and telling them to trust in Jesus. But they spend the majority of their lives on the Greek road, so they don't understand or respond to the message!

Sadly, most churches today are not teaching their young people how to defend their faith. They don't understand the true history recorded in Scripture that is foundational to all doctrines and the gospel. Most churches are not teaching apologetics (how to answer the skeptical questions of this age). Because of this, so many kids are growing up doubting, not defending the Bible as the infallible Word of God. The research Answers in Genesis had conducted by America's Research Group[1] clearly showed that questions about creation, evolution, age of earth, dinosaurs, Noah's Ark, the Flood, Garden of Eden, etc., were a major cause of why so many young people were leaving the

1. Ken Ham, Britt Beemer, and Todd Hillard, *Already Gone: Why Your Kids Will Quit Church and What You Can Do to Stop it* (Green Forest, AR: Master Books, 2016).

Church by the time they reached college age. Their churches weren't teaching apologetics to equip them with answers. Instead, someone else was teaching them apologetics — but *false* apologetics.

Most students attend public (state-run) schools where teachers and their textbooks teach apologetics to defend evolution, millions of years, and naturalism (atheism). By and large, at many churches these students are taught what are called Bible "stories," instead of teaching them the Bible as factual history. But at public (state) school (and sadly many so-called Christian/Church schools), they hear something like this: "Here are the reasons the Bible's account in Genesis is not true. Here is the evidence for evolution. This is the evidence for millions of years." And in many churches they often hear, "You can believe all that you're taught at school about evolution and millions of years, but trust in Jesus anyway!" Most of the Church leaders have taken the supposed millions of years and basically said, "We'll fit these millions of years into the Bible in the 'days' of creation, or in a gap between the first two verses, or in some way fit it into the Bible before the creation of man."

But here's a major problem. As soon as one believes in millions of years, then you have allowed death, bloodshed, and disease (as exhibited in the fossil record) to exist *before* Adam sinned.

The Bible teaches us in Genesis 1:29–30 that Adam and Eve and the animals were originally vegetarians:

> And God said, "Behold, I have given you every plant yielding seed that is on the face of all the earth, and every tree with seed in its fruit. You shall have them for food. And to every beast of the earth and to every bird of the heavens and to everything that creeps on the earth, everything that has the breath of life, I have given every green plant for food." And it was so.

Humans weren't even told they could eat meat until *after* the Flood in Genesis 9:3:

> Every moving thing that lives shall be food for you. And as I gave you the green plants, I give you everything.

But the fossil record is replete with examples of animals eating animals, bones in their stomachs, etc.

In the fossil record, there are also examples of brain tumors, cancer, and arthritis in various skeletons. If these things existed before Adam sinned, then there's an insurmountable problem because after God made Adam and Eve, He said everything was "very good."

> And God saw everything that he had made, and behold, it was very good. And there was evening and there was morning, the sixth day (Genesis 1:31).

If millions of years occurred prior to God creating Adam, this would mean that God called cancer "very good." There are also thorns in the fossil record claimed by evolutionists to be hundreds of millions of years old. Yet the Bible states clearly that thorns came *after* the Curse.

> ... thorns and thistles it shall bring forth for you; and you shall eat the plants of the field (Genesis 3:18).

The Bible makes very clear that death, bloodshed, disease, and suffering are a consequence of sin and the Curse. First came sin, then the resulting Curse of sin: disease, death, suffering, etc. However, if a Christian believes in millions of years, then they must also believe all these existed *before* sin. And this would flatly contradict the entire Word of God. For how can one believe in death and disease before sin when the Bible clearly teaches death and disease are a consequence of sin? These cannot both be true at the same time! This is a major reason why "Theistic Evolution," or old-earth, God-guided evolution, is an oxymoron and why no Bible-believing Christian should embrace such a lie.

This means, if the Bible is right (and it is), those fossil layers with all the dead things in them and evidence of disease had to form *after* sin. Does the Bible give us a clue as to how fossil layers could have been formed all over the earth after sin? Yes — the Flood of Noah's day. Most of the fossil record is actually evidence of the graveyard of the Flood of Noah's day. It's not the graveyard of millions of years before humans.

This presents a huge dilemma for the Church. We have generations of kids who have been told by the media, education system, and most of our Church leaders that death has always been here for millions of years. They are not taught the Genesis account of history as literal truth. They don't understand that our sin in Adam brought death into the world. So, consequently, they really don't understand the sacrificial system that pointed toward the ultimate sacrifice in Christ. Is it any wonder that many fail to understand how we (because of our sin in Adam) messed up the world and now it's groaning because of our sin? Look at what Paul wrote to the Romans:

> For the creation was subjected to futility, not willingly, but because of him who subjected it, in hope that the creation itself will be set free from its bondage to corruption and obtain the freedom of the glory of the children of God. For we know that the whole creation has been groaning together in the pains of childbirth until now. And not only the creation, but we ourselves, who have the firstfruits of the Spirit, groan inwardly as we wait eagerly for adoption as sons, the redemption of our bodies (Romans 8:20–23).

Coming generations, for the most part, don't understand the holiness of God and what sin really is. They

For we know that the whole creation has been groaning together in the pains of childbirth until now.

ROMANS 8:22 ESV

are all confused. That's why many think that if you are a good person, you can get to heaven. Many won't oppose gay "marriage." They are so used to taking man's ideas like "millions of years" and adding that to God's Word, so they take man's ideas about marriage and add that to God's Word as well. They have been taught that one's feelings determine truth, and it's all about love. No! It's all about what God's Word clearly teaches. Most of our kids today are very "Greek" in their thinking because of the indoctrination in secular beliefs.

Many in my generation would never have thought there would be a time in our Western world when the Bible would be accused of being a book of hate speech and be so "outlawed" from a culture. And yet, this is starting to happen in our Western world. In Canada, they have told Christian schools that they can't use parts of the Bible because it is hate speech. In Australia, the United Kingdom, and the USA, the free exercise of Christianity is increasingly being stonewalled. In these nations, when Christians speak up against gay "marriage," gender fluidity, or abortion, it is considered "hate speech," and attempts are being made to try to outlaw such speech.

So here is a lesson for Christians who believe that marriage is for one man and one woman (as taught in Genesis 2 and confirmed by Jesus in Matthew 19 and Mark 10). When talking with someone who believes in gay "marriage," if you try to impose your view of marriage on them and they don't have the foundation of God's Word and the history in Genesis where God made marriage as a union between male and female, then it won't work. They lack the foundation for such a biblical worldview! It's like trying to build a house by starting with the roof.

That's why you can't ultimately legislate morality. It's a worldview issue that flows out of your foundation, either from God's Word or man's word. It's a spiritual issue. Those with a man-based foundation will have a different worldview from those whose foundation comes from Scripture. This is why we view moral issues differently. What is morally "right" to one will not necessarily be "right" to the other. Christians with a moral foundation coming from God's Word will often clash with those whose foundation is built on human reasoning.

WHAT CAUSED
THE GREAT DIVIDE?

Back in 2010, *Free Inquiry*, a secular humanist magazine, stated,

> A historic transition is occurring. Barely noticed, slowly, quietly, imperceptibly, religion [when they say "religion," they usually mean Christianity] is shriveling in America, as it already has in Europe, Canada, Australia, across the developed world. Increasingly, supernatural faith belongs to the third world. The first world is entering the long-predicted secular age where science and knowledge dominate.[1]

---

1. James A. Haught, "Fading Faith," *Free Inquiry* 30, no. 2 (February/March 2010).

What they are saying is that there's been a change in our Western world from an Acts 2 culture to an Acts 17 one. Do you know who really helped facilitate this change, escalating it in a big way? President Barack Obama. While he was still a Senator, Obama spoke in 2006 at a conference called "Building a Covenant for a New America."

In his keynote speech, Obama talked about "a new America."[2] Here's what he said back at that time:

Whatever we once were, we are no longer a Christian nation. At least not *just*. We are also a Jewish nation, a Muslim nation, and a Buddhist nation, and a Hindu nation and a nation of non-believers.[3]

This became one of Obama's mantras, which is repeated in his book, *The Audacity of Hope*. He said something similar to the president of Turkey when he

2. Barack Obama, keynote speech, delivered at Sojourners/Call to Renewal's "Building a Covenant for a New America" conference, Washington, DC, June 26, 2006.

3. Ibid.

visited there. He made similar statements many times during his eight years in office. When we look now at what happened during the eight years of his presidency, we can see what he meant by "a new America."

I believe he was actually saying, "We are no longer a nation that believes in one God and builds our thinking on the Bible."

That's what he wanted to let everyone know, that he was going to fundamentally transform the predominant worldview of our nation from a Christianized one to a secular one. This is the change from an Acts 2-type culture to an Acts 17-type culture. Obama said America was now a nation that has many gods. Many of the Founding Fathers were Christian, and many of those who weren't Christian still respected the Bible. The predominant worldview that permeated America since its inception came from the Bible. That worldview included a belief that marriage was between one man and one woman, and that murdering babies was wrong. People understood right and wrong because there was an absolute authority — the Word of God. If people don't build their thinking on God's Word, there's only one other foundation, and that's man's word. When there's no absolute authority to declare what is absolutely right and wrong, we end up like ancient Israel during the time of the Judges.

> In those days there was no king in Israel.
> Everyone did what was right in his own eyes
> (Judges 21:25).

The moral relativism that afflicted Israel is happening now in America. America was once an Acts 2-type culture where most people (consciously or unconsciously) had the starting point of God's Word for their worldview. This is why a Christian worldview permeated our culture. However, America is now much more like an Acts 17-type culture, where the starting point is predominantly man's word. As a result, we see moral relativism pervading the culture. That's the change that has occurred, but tragically most in the Church don't understand why this has happened.

WHERE DID THE
CHURCH GO WRONG?

Why did the Church not see this coming? In 2009, *Newsweek* magazine featured this head-line on its cover: "The Decline and Fall of Christian America."[1] Even secular media saw it happening before our very eyes, and yet many in the Church seemed to have little understanding of the cause and nature of this radical change.

"The present, in this sense, is less about the death of God and more about the birth of many gods."[2]

---

1. Jon Meacham, "The End of Christian America," *Newsweek*, April 13, 2009, p. 36.
2. Ibid.

I believe some people's view of eschatology (the study of the end times) affected their response to America's moral decline. For instance, I have had a number of people tell me something like this: "Well, that's to be expected, as in the last days, things are going to get worse!" And then they stated, "Oh well! Let it happen! Bring it on!"

But this is more *fatalism* than biblical eschatology. They reason, "So, what's the point of trying to do anything?" They think the worse it gets, the more likely Jesus is coming back again soon, so Christians just need to sit back and wait! But nowhere in Scripture does the truth about Jesus' return inspire such a response. In fact, it's just the opposite! It's when we find ourselves in the midst of a "crooked and perverse generation" that we are to appear as "lights *in* the world" (Philippians 2:15, emphasis added). Paul told the Romans that the truth about the coming of the Lord is motivation to "wake up" and "put on the armor of light," *not* to sit around passively and let culture go to hell. To do nothing is a misapplication and an inappropriate response to eschatology and Bible prophecy. As things get darker in culture, the Church must shine all the more brightly in society. It's an opportunity to work, not an excuse to "wait."

No matter what's going on in the culture, we need to be doing what God has clearly instructed us to do. We're to be about the business of the King, preaching the Gospel, giving answers, and contending for the faith (Matthew 28:18–20; Acts 1:8; 1 Peter 3:15; Jude 1:3).

> ... but sanctify Christ as Lord in your hearts, always being ready to make a defense to everyone who asks you to give an account for the hope that is in you, yet with gentleness and reverence (1 Peter 3:15; NASB).

Of course, we are in the last days (e.g., Acts 2:17; Hebrews 1:2; etc.)! We just don't know exactly how "last" we are. All we really know is that it's later than it's ever been before! We don't know when Christ will return. I've had people tell me that today's culture is like that of the days of Noah before the judgment came. However, I disagree. I don't think the culture is as bad as it was in the days of Noah. The Bible makes it clear that only eight people went through the door of the Ark to be saved. And this is what God's Word states about the rest of the population of the earth at that time:

> The LORD saw that the wickedness of man was great in the earth, and that every

> intention of the thoughts of his heart was
> only evil continually (Genesis 6:5).

Now we do observe rampant sin in our culture. And in many ways, I believe Romans 1 is a description of what is happening in our Western world. But there's still an enormous remnant of on-fire Christians in America. And although the percentages are small, there is quite a number of Christians in other Western countries. Even though there is increasing Christian persecution throughout the world and the sin of abortion and rejection of God's Word concerning marriage and gender is rampant, our culture is not yet like it was in the days of Sodom and Gomorrah. Remember, God would have saved Sodom if there were ten righteous people — but there weren't even ten!

> Then he [Abraham] said, "Oh let not
> the Lord be angry, and I will speak again
> but this once. Suppose ten are found there."
> He answered, "For the sake of ten I will not
> destroy it." And the LORD went his way,
> when he had finished speaking to Abraham,
> and Abraham returned to his place
> (Genesis 18:32–33).

So, shouldn't we be doing what the Bible says, and do business (occupy) until He comes?

Calling ten of his servants, he gave them ten minas, and said to them, "Engage in business until I come" (Luke 19:13).

And that means we are to be doing what God's Word instructs:

1. Contend for the Faith.

Beloved, although I was very eager to write to you about our common salvation, I found it necessary to write appealing to you to contend for the faith that was once for all delivered to the saints (Jude 1:3).

2. Give answers for what you believe.

… but in your hearts honor Christ the Lord as holy, always being prepared to make a defense to anyone who asks you for a reason for the hope that is in you; yet do it with gentleness and respect (1 Peter 3:15).

3. Preach the Gospel.

And he said to them, "Go into all the world and proclaim the gospel to the whole creation" (Mark 16:15).

That theology drove me to respond, "We should build a creation museum." And then, "Yes, let's build an Ark." I believe we should do whatever we can to reach people with the message of God's Word and the saving gospel. Of course, some Christians told me these were ridiculous ideas because Jesus was going to come back any time, and we wouldn't even get these facilities finished. I'm glad I didn't listen to people's opinions but instead took God's Word seriously! Millions of people are now being influenced by these two leading Christian attractions. You see, Jesus might not come back for another 1,000 years. Or maybe another 500 years. Or maybe next week. Or tomorrow. We don't know. We're told we don't know the day or the hour. But we are to do whatever we can to do the business of our King, which includes spreading the truth of God's Word and the salvation message to the best of our abilities.

Another problem in the church is that many of our Christian leaders, Sunday school teachers, and parents have got a foot on both sides of the widening chasm — straddling between the "Greek" side and the "Jewish" side. Many in the Church try to marry man's beliefs with God's Word. But with the chasm widening so rapidly, they are going to have to decide which side they are on. Like Joshua, we must declare,

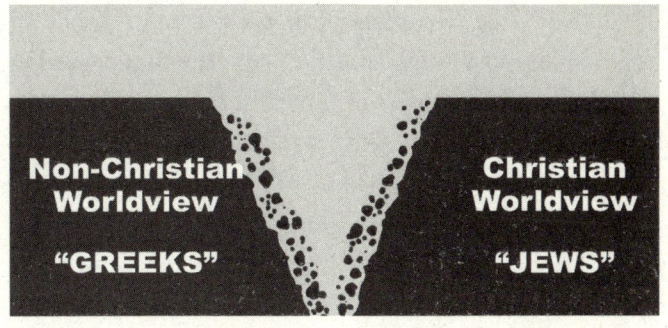

"If it is disagreeable in your sight to serve the LORD, choose for yourselves today whom you will serve: whether the gods which your fathers served which were beyond the River, or the gods of the Amorites in whose land you are living; but as for me and my house, we will serve the LORD" (Joshua 24:15; NASB).

I have even been to churches in the Southern "Bible Belt" area of the United States where a pastor will tell me I will be "preaching to the choir" in his church because they all believe the Bible. I've heard the pastor get up in front of me and say something like, "We believe the Bible in this church, from Genesis to Revelation. I told Ken Ham he's 'speaking to the choir,' as we are a Bible-believing fundamentalist church."

Then I get up and speak on the importance of taking Genesis literally and that all Christian doctrines are ultimately founded in Genesis. I challenge people that they could not compromise Genesis with evolutionary ideas and millions of years. Afterward, the people ask me questions, such as, "Where did Cain get his wife?" "What about carbon-dating?" "Do you think dinosaurs really existed?" "Could Noah really get all those animals on the Ark?" "Doesn't the millions of years fit in a gap between the first two verses of Genesis?" And many similar kinds of questions about Genesis.

Do you know why they ask all those questions? Because they are all really "Greeks" in their thinking about this topic. And I find the pastor is "Greek" also because he went to a "Greek" seminary. Most of these seminaries compromise Genesis in one way or another. I've had so many pastors tell me they were never taught how to answer questions about Genesis, evolution, millions of years, etc. — so they avoid the topic when teaching their congregations.

I also find many in the Church ask me why their kids/grandkids who were brought up in the church aren't going to church anymore! I then explain from my experience that a major factor is that they were educated to be "Greeks" and weren't taught the

Newsweek article

answers to the accusations they heard that science supposedly disproved the Genesis account.

Actually, the whole world is really "Greek" to one degree or another. All of us, to some extent, have been influenced by this "Greek" way of thinking.

If you want to deal with this growing chasm in the culture, then the only solution is the saving gospel of Jesus Christ. However, for this to effectively happen, the gospel must be presented in a way that those hearing the message will understand. In the *Newsweek*[3] magazine I referred to earlier, there was one sentence that stood out to me more than any other:

> The present, in this sense, is less about the death of God and more about the birth of many gods.

Instead of one God, now there are many gods. I believe this was exactly what President Obama was saying. But much of the Church is still trying to preach Acts 2 sermons to an Acts 17 culture.

---

3 Jon Meacham, "The End of Christian America," *Newsweek*, April 13, 2009.

THE SOLUTION —
A GOSPEL RESET

So, going back to Acts 17 and Paul's preaching to the Greeks, how could he explain the Gospel to them so that they understood it? How could he build the right sort of "house" so it would stand? He would need to remove any wrong foundation and then construct the right foundation so the structure could be built. The Greek culture had the wrong foundation of man's word instead of God's Word. Paul would need to explain, starting at the very beginning, the correct history, and ensure they understood terms like *God* and *sin* so they could comprehend the message. And that's precisely what he did! Many miss this important point because they are not looking at the big picture here concerning

Paul's response to the Greeks' non-understanding of the message of the gospel.

When he went to Mars Hill, looked around, and saw all these altars and temples they had, he noticed the altar to the unknown god. He basically said, "Let me tell you who He is," and then he defined the Creator God of the Bible:

> So Paul, standing in the midst of the Areopagus, said: "Men of Athens, I perceive that in every way you are very religious. For as I passed along and observed the objects of your worship, I found also an altar with this inscription: 'To the unknown god.' What therefore you worship as unknown, this I proclaim to you. The God who made the world and everything in it, being Lord of heaven and earth, does not live in temples made by man, nor is he served by human hands, as though he needed anything, since he himself gives to all mankind life and breath and everything. And he made from one man every nation of mankind to live on all the face of the earth, having determined allotted periods and the boundaries of their dwelling place, that they should seek God, and perhaps feel their way toward him and find him" (Acts 17:22–27).

Mars Hill

Paul began with the "ABC's" (**A**lways **B**een a **C**reator). He explained that the one true God made the world and everything in it. He's the Lord of heaven, and He doesn't dwell in temples made with hands. He doesn't need things, but rather He provides all things. All people are of one blood, from one man, so we are all one race. Observational science has actually confirmed there's only one "race." This was confirmed when the Human Genome Project mapped the human genome and released their results to the world in 2000.[1] Yes, there's only one race, but different people groups because of the Tower of Babel. This is what we teach at the Creation Museum and the Ark Encounter attractions. We do this so people can understand we're all descendants of Adam, thus all sinners, and all in need of a Savior. This is, in essence, what Paul was relating to the Greeks.

In a sense, Paul was saying, "Let me give you the right starting point and get you on the right road so that you can understand the message of the Cross."

---

1. National Human Genome Research Institute, "International Human Genome Sequencing Consortium Announces 'Working Draft' of Human Genome," *National Human Genome Research Institute*, https://www.genome.gov/10001457/2000-release-working-draft-of-human-genome-sequence/, accessed January 4, 2018.

When we read Romans, what do we find? When Paul explains the gospel and talks about sin and death, he refers back to the history in Genesis:

> Therefore, just as sin came into the world through one man, and death through sin, and so death spread to all men because all sinned (Romans 5:12).

> Thus it is written, "The first man Adam became a living being"; the last Adam became a life-giving spirit (1 Corinthians 15:45).

When Paul talked to the Greeks about God in Acts 17, he didn't use the Jewish word *Jehovah*, but rather the Greek word *Theos*. He did this in order to more effectively communicate to them.

JEWS	**GREEKS**
ACTS 2—PETER	ACTS 17—PAUL
☑ God	☒ Which God?
☑ Sin	☒ What sin?
☑ Death	☒ Why death?
☒ Savior	☒ Why savior?

In a culture that is like the Jewish one (an Acts 2 culture), when you say "God," they understand the one Creator God. When you use words like *sin*, they understand because they have the history of the Fall of man. They know that death is the penalty for sin. They understand the sacrificial system and that God promised the Messiah would come. However, their stumbling block is that Jesus is the Messiah and He came as the babe in a manger.

This is where our Western culture used to be — very much an Acts 2-type culture. But now we have an Acts 17-type culture that has no foundation in the history of the Fall or a biblical understanding of sin. Their stumbling block is that, without that foundation, the Word seems like foolishness.

Now, when you compare a creation-based culture (like the Jews) with an evolution-based culture (like the Greeks), you're essentially comparing America of yesteryear to the America of today. And this is what is happening throughout Western culture. This is the divide we are experiencing. And that divide is widening quickly.

The "Greeks" are on the wrong road because they have the wrong starting point. This is the battle that began in the Garden 6,000 years ago, a war between God's Word and man's word. It's a battle over two starting points that puts people on two different roads. The starting point of God's Word puts one on the road that leads up to the message of the Cross. The starting point of man's word puts one on a road that leads only to destruction (Matthew 7:13). One is narrow and the other is wide (Matthew 7:13–14).

The "Greek road" does not lead up to the message of the Cross, so how would you get the "Greek" to understand the message of the Cross? You would have to take them off the wrong road, give them the right starting point, and put them on the right road, with the right beginning, that leads to the message of the Cross.

We need to present the gospel the way God does in the Bible by starting at the beginning. Now, that's a radical idea: start at the beginning! Maybe that's why

God called the first book in the Bible Genesis (which means *beginning*)! Actually, this is why God gives us a detailed history from the beginning through to the end — from Genesis to Revelation.

There's nothing new under the sun (Ecclesiastes 1:9). When I went to Japan a number of years ago, my Japanese translator said something like this:

> You've got to be careful over here, because there is no Christian basis to speak of. If you use the word "God," because of their Shinto-ism and belief in thousands of gods, they're going to think you're speaking about just another god like all the others. These people don't know what sin is, as they don't have the teaching from Genesis in their culture. Here's the problem — you've got to define your terms. You will have to define what you mean by *God* and *sin*. You'll need to teach them why and when death entered the world. Actually, you have to start at the beginning and explain the foundation of the gospel beginning in Genesis.

I realized that the Japanese culture was really an illustration of the Acts 17 culture, and I had to preach the message by starting at the beginning, so they would

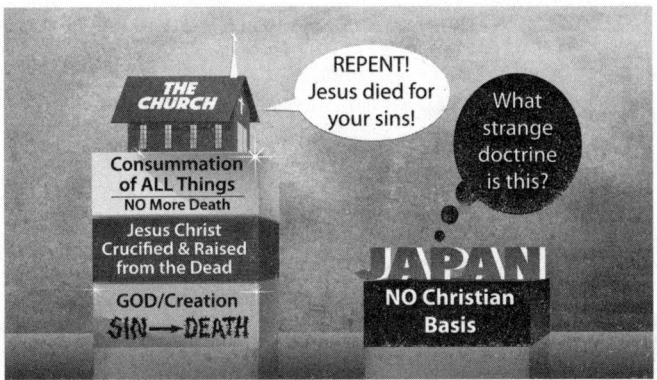

understand it. We have to do the same thing today in Western culture.

At the Creation Museum, we explain the two different starting points, and by doing so, put each visitor on the right road. We start with the foundation of God's Word, beginning in Genesis. Then we walk you through the Bible from the beginning to the end. This enables us to explain the gospel from the foundation up.

Once we go through that anthropological, astronomical, biological, and geological history in the Bible, we explain how this history is true and confirmed by science. We then present the message of Christ, Cross, and Consummation that's founded in that history.

Through the Answers in Genesis ministry, we are challenging generations today by helping them understand that many of them are on the wrong road, and we want to do our best to get them on the right road. That's what Paul did. Once he pointed them to the right starting point and the right road, then he went back to preaching the message he began with — the message of the Resurrection. When he did this initially, they didn't understand, and his message was foolishness to them. But after explaining the true God from the right starting point, we see three different responses:

(1) Some mocked, just like last time, but (2) others started to listen, and (3) a few believed. Now some Christians/Christian leaders claim Paul wasn't very successful, while others strongly suggest he was phenomenally successful. Think about it. He was dealing with an outright pagan culture that didn't have a clue about the truth of God's Word and had the wrong foundation. Some actually believed and others wanted to hear more! It would be similar to Christians today preaching to a college campus full of ardent atheists.

Sadly, there are Church leaders today who tell people to only use the Acts 2 approach and be like Peter and just preach the message of the Cross and Resurrection. They tell people not to use the method Paul used in Acts 17, as they claim he was very intellectual about his faith, so he only saw a few converts. I suggest that Paul was extremely successful and that we should follow his example.

Here's the point: Peter was going to the Jews, but Paul was going to Greeks. That's the difference. Paul, in a sense, had to turn "Greeks" into "Jews." He had to approach people who had a wrong foundation and a wrong worldview and then give them a totally different foundation with a totally different worldview.

Imagine a builder coming to build a house and finding that someone has already constructed a foundation — but it's the wrong one. The first thing the builder has to do is demolish the wrong foundation and build a different but correct foundation upon which to build that house. That's what Paul did with the Greeks.

CONCLUSION

America, the United Kingdom, and Australia were once cultures like the Jewish one in Acts 2. When someone preached repentance to them, they understood the message. But what's been happening is there has been a widening separation between a Christianized worldview and a non-Christian, secular worldview. And this secular worldview is permeating coming generations. That's the divide we see happening in America (and our whole Western world) right now. Some in the media are calling it a civil war. It is a war, but a spiritual one that has been raging for 6,000 years. Sadly, there is a rapidly increasing number of soldiers in the army of the "Greeks" and depleting numbers in the army of the "Jews."

Many of those in America in the older generations who are still like the "Jews" are not necessarily

Christians, though many were brought up in the Church, and many still do attend church. They don't really understand what is happening, even though they have a Christianized worldview. However, they do perceive a massive change in our culture, and many are perplexed and even horrified by it.

In this era, I earnestly believe we need to do a lot of what I call "de-Greekizing" of people, so they will be able to listen and understand the gospel. Not only do we need to start our message at the beginning in Genesis, but we need to deal with the false information that generations have been taught that makes so many doubt and disbelieve the Bible. We have to be equipped with answers and be ready to give a defense of faith against the onslaught of evolutionary teaching that has permeated people's thinking around the world. If we are going to evangelize the culture, we do need to understand there has been an incredible attack on the "Book" — God's written Word.

Let me put it this way. It's as if the devil has said, "You Christians can go on teaching kids about the miracles Jesus did in the New Testament. You can teach them about the babe in a manger, and the Resurrection. You can teach them about Jesus healing blind people and raising the dead. Teach them about the feeding of the 5,000, about the Israelites crossing the Red Sea, about Jonah being in a great fish for three days. Go ahead. Teach them these stories. And while you are doing that, I'm going to be indoctrinating those same kids *not* to believe the Book. I'm going to use the fake news of evolution and millions of years to brainwash them into believing science has effectively disproved the Bible, making it nothing more than an outdated, obsolete book of 'stories.' And since you won't be teaching apologetics, I will teach my own apologetics through the education systems, media, and the Internet to make sure they doubt God's Word. The more this happens, most won't even listen to your message of the gospel."

We are now in an age where generations have been heavily inoculated against the Bible. We have to deal with this crisis, pointing them to God's Word — starting at the beginning, so they will understand the Gospel. It's sort of like the parable of the sower and the seed. When the sower threw out seed, he knew there were different types of ground out there. Years ago, you could assume there was lots of plowed ground that I call "Acts 2 ground." But there's hardly any Acts 2 ground left at all now in our Western world. Christians are out there today, throwing out the seed the way they've spread the Gospel in the past, saying in essence, "These weeds are getting worse every day, these kids aren't responding. Oh well, we'll keep throwing out the seed."

But because of compromise and lack of teaching of apologetics, much of the Church has allowed the once Acts 2 (plowed) ground to become Acts 17 ground that is covered in rocks, trees, and weeds (representing evolution, millions of years, etc.). Some refer to this as a "post-Christian culture." And in some ways, we are becoming even "pre-Christian." Before the seed can be planted, we need to clear the ground and plow it, so the seed (the gospel) can take root to enable a harvest (of souls).

When the pioneers in America traveled westward, they didn't just place their wagons in a circle, throw out seed, and wait for the harvest. They had to prepare the ground before they could plant the seed. We are in a situation analogous to those pioneers, where we can't assume there's plowed ground as there once was. We can't assume they will easily receive the seed leading to a spiritual harvest. Instead, we have to work at plowing the ground first, so that we *can* plant the seed. We need to go out and "de-Greekize."

Practical De-Greekizing

After speaking at a conference, a young man came up to me and said something like, "I'm a homosexual and believe in 'gay marriage,' what do you think about that?"

Now some Christians would tell this person that homosexual behavior is sin and they need to repent. However, I would not respond this way. I recognize that I can't impose my worldview on someone that doesn't have the same foundation I have. I first of all need to understand this person's starting point for the worldview they have.

If I find out this person admits they are not a Christian, I then tell them I want to explain why I have the worldview I do concerning how I approach the issue of homosexuality and gay "marriage."

I told this person that I start with the Bible as the foundation of my thinking. The man responded that he doesn't believe the Bible and rejects what he called "religion." So I then related to him that even though he doesn't believe the Bible, I do, and I would like to know why he doesn't believe it is the revealed Word of God as I do. In this instance, the young man said that science had disproved the Bible. So then I asked him to give me some examples that illustrate this so I could have the opportunity to answer them.

What I was doing was giving him answers to help him understand why I could defend my position that the Bible was what it claimed to be — the revealed Word of God that gives what I believe to be the true account of the origin of the universe and life, written by the One who knows everything there is to know about everything. We continued this discussion for a while, and then I said I wanted to show him how I build my worldview on the details that are given in the Bible, particularly in the first 11 chapters of Genesis.

I was then able to summarize the account of the creation of Adam from dust, Eve from his side, and explain that this was the first marriage. Also, I used Matthew 19 and Mark 10 to show that the creation account of Adam and Eve was quoted in the New Testament as the foundation for marriage being one man and one woman. Then I told him that if he didn't have the same foundation as me, but believed man evolved by natural processes and rejected the God of the Bible, I could totally understand why he believed the way he did. He started to understand that the clash between us really wasn't about how we viewed marriage or homosexuality — it was actually a clash over the difference between our starting points for our worldview.

I was then able to explain the gospel, beginning in Genesis with the creation of Adam and Eve, the Fall of man and thus the entrance of sin and death, and thus establish the need for a Savior. We did discuss other questions he had relating to supposed reasons the Bible was disproved in our scientific age. So, my approach was to assume this person had no understanding of the foundation needed to comprehend a Christian worldview. Sadly, this is increasingly the situation with the coming generations in our very secularized culture.

Now if this young man had claimed he was a Christian, I would then challenge such a person from the Bible, beginning in Genesis, concerning the origin and meaning of marriage. When I do this I find they will usually tell me they don't take Genesis literally like I do. Then I ask questions to find out why they approach Genesis the way they do — and usually I find out they too have issues concerning what they claim are scientific evidences that disprove Genesis as literal history. I then pursue dealing with these so-called evidences, to do my best to help them understand science has not disproved the Bible. Then I will deal with what the Bible claims of itself, so we can discuss what it means that it is God's Word.

My point is that we can no longer assume the people we are talking to will understand Christian terminology, or why Christians believe the way they do. In fact, many just have little or no understanding of the true gospel and what constitutes a Christian way of thinking. We need to understand where they are coming from, why they believe what they do, and know how to converse with them so they don't get the idea we are trying to impose what we believe on them. Instead, we need to help them understand why they believe the way they do from their starting point, and then teach them what Christians believe and why. At the same time we will need to be answering questions they pose along the way as objections to why the Bible and the Christian message can be trusted.

Yes, we live in a very different world. As I said at the beginning, the gospel message hasn't changed, but the way in which it needs to be presented in a secularized culture does need to change. The way to present the gospel does need to be reset in the world we now live in.

The ministry of Answers of Genesis understands this need to reset, and has produced unique but powerful resources to do just that.

Resources

At Answers in Genesis (AiG), we have created a four-year Sunday school curriculum ranging from pre-kindergarten through adult that is totally synchronized. It's called "Answers Bible Curriculum." A — for Apologetics. B — for Biblical Authority. C — for Chronological. The teaching begins at the beginning, starting with Genesis, and then going chronologically through the entire Bible. Old and New Testaments are connected as the teaching progresses, and apologetics is taught all the way through, equipping students with answers to the questions they will hear or accusations against the Bible that they may need to deal with. As of this writing, over 10,000 churches are using this unique powerful curriculum, with pastors and others telling us it is revolutionizing their churches. Many pastors have said that this curriculum has resulted in reversing the exodus from the Church that was occurring in the younger generations. Sadly, a lot of Sunday school material today can only be described as "fluff and stuff." AiG's ABC Curriculum is very "meaty." And kids of all ages tell us they love the in-depth teaching.

Answers in Genesis also produces a VBS program used by thousands of churches. Each VBS program deals with biblical doctrine, apologetics, and a clear presentation of the gospel. Churches are testifying that when using the AiG VBS program they've seen an exciting increase in the number of kids (and even adults) committing their lives to the Lord Jesus Christ.

For more information on other resources and the two leading Christian attractions in the world, The Creation Museum and the Ark Encounter, go to:

> Answersingenesis.org
> Creationmuseum.org
> Arkencounter.com

Appendix A
Genesis–Romans Road

Genesis 1:1 — God made everything.

In the beginning God created the heavens and the earth.

Genesis 1:31 — God made everything perfectly — no death or suffering.

Then God saw everything that He had made, and indeed it was very good. So the evening and the morning were the sixth day.

Genesis 3:17–19 — The punishment for sin is death; due to sin, the world is no longer perfect.

Then to Adam He said, "Because you have heeded the voice of your wife, and have eaten from the tree of which I commanded you, saying, 'You shall not eat of it': Cursed is the ground for your sake; in toil you shall eat of it all the days of your life. Both thorns and thistles it shall bring forth for you, and you shall eat the herb of the field. In the sweat of your face you shall eat bread till you return to the ground, for out of it you were taken; for dust you are, and to dust you shall return."

Romans 5:12 — Because our mutual grandfather Adam sinned, we now sin too.

Therefore, just as through one man sin entered the world, and death through sin, and thus death spread to all men, because all sinned.

Romans 3:23 — We need to realize all are sinners, including ourselves.

For all have sinned and fall short of the glory of God.

Romans 10:9 — We must trust in Jesus Christ as Savior and Lord.

If you confess with your mouth that Jesus is Lord and believe in your heart that God raised him from the dead, you will be saved.

Appendix B
Unlocking the Door

I want to briefly illustrate how Christians "unlocked a door" that has been progressively pushed open in generation after generation. The result today in our Western world is a weakened church.

For instance, among U.S. teenagers today who call themselves born-again Christians, only 9% believe there is such a thing as absolute truth![1] The church is, by and large, no longer influencing the culture in our once very Christianized West, but now the culture is rapidly influencing (infiltrating) the church.

When one considers nations like the United Kingdom, America, Canada, New Zealand, and Australia, there is no doubt that these cultures were once much more Christian (e.g., in their worldview, morality) than they are today.

Consider the USA. In our modern era, this country has certainly been the greatest Christianized nation on earth. It still has the greatest number of churches, Bible colleges, Christian colleges, seminaries, Christian radio, TV stations, and Christian bookshops in the entire world. More than half of the world's missionaries are sent out from America.[2]

And yet, for all the Christian influence within and emanating from this country, the culture is becoming less Christianized (in fact more anti-Christian) every day.[3] I believe the church progressively adopted "Baconian" philosophy (named for Francis Bacon, who, though a professed Christian, was influential for this movement — he also described the scientific method), thus leading to this situation.

In John 3:12, Jesus states the following: "If I have told you earthly things and you do not believe, how can you believe if I tell you heavenly things?" Let me apply this verse in a particular way. If one can't believe the earthly things spoken of in the Bible (e.g., the history in Genesis, which encompasses biology, physics, astronomy, geology, anthropology, etc.), then how can one believe the spiritual things (e.g., morality and the message of salvation), which are based in this "earthly" history?

One reason the genealogies are listed in such detail in various parts of the Bible is to help teach us the real history, beginning in Genesis (including the first Adam and the origin of sin and death), and going through to the "last Adam" (1 Corinthians 15:45 — the Lord Jesus Christ, the Son of God, who stepped into history to save us from our sin). If the record of this *history* can't be trusted, neither can the message of morality and salvation that is based in this history. If there was no literal first Adam and the Fall (original sin), and death as a consequence, what is the meaning of the "last Adam" and Christ's death and Resurrection? If God's Word is not infallible, then God is not the absolute authority. Who, therefore, determines absolutes concerning morality?

Much of the church has adopted the spiritual teachings of the Bible (the message of morality and salvation — even that is somewhat questionable today with so much compromise on Genesis in the church!), but has rejected a significant amount of its history. The Bible is, to most, a book of stories containing important "truths." But the history (particularly in the early chapters of Genesis) is not viewed as important — or even real.

Consider the following conversation, which represents many I have had with audiences in the USA, UK, and Australia.

I ask them, "If I were to ask the average Sunday school teacher this question, 'In Sunday school, do you teach biology, geology, astronomy, anthropology and chemistry?" — what would the answer be?"

The audience responds, "No."

I then ask, "If I asked, 'What do you teach in Sunday school then?'" — what would the teacher say?"

The audience replies, "About Jesus — about the Bible."

I then continue, "Okay, now if I asked, 'Where do students learn about biology, geology, astronomy, anthropology, physics, and chemistry?'" — what would the Sunday school teacher say?"

The answer I receive is always a resounding, "At school!"

And my response? "Oh, I get it. At Sunday school (in fact in most church programs) we teach about Jesus and the Bible, but at school, students learn about geology, biology etc." I explain that statistics show that around 90 percent of students from church homes in America (probably a higher figure in other countries) still go to government schools.[4] The Barna Research Group estimates that nearly 70 percent of teens and young adults from churched homes leave the church upon leaving home.[5]

Why is this so? What is happening? It basically is like this. At church, students (and adults) are taught about Jesus and other stories (Jonah and the great sea creature; feeding the 5,000; Paul's missionary journeys, etc.), whereas at school, they are taught what they have been increasingly led to believe is the real history of the world in regard to geology, biology, astronomy, etc.

This "real" history the world teaches encompasses such things as the earth is billions of years old; man evolved from ape-like ancestors; the Bible has nothing to do with science; the "big bang" brought the universe into existence; there was no Adam and Eve; there was no Fall into sin; the evidence of animals changing (by mutation and natural selection) is deceptively equated with molecules-to-man evolution; the Bible teaches religion, but schools teach "real" science; etc.

In other words, the reality is that progressively, generation after generation, students have been conditioned to see the Bible as something that deals with morality and salvation, but what they are taught at school deals with supposed "real" history. It has been a subtle switch of religions in the school systems, secular media, and secular museums — from a Christian worldview to a secular humanistic religion.

But the history recorded of the beginning in the Bible does involve biology, geology, astronomy, physics, anthropology, and chemistry. Now, the Bible is not a science textbook per se (which is a good thing, since science textbooks change every year!). But the Bible is a revelation of history that gives us the "Big Picture" in every area of reality. In other words, the Bible gives us the right foundational thinking, so we can approach geology, biology, anthropology, etc. in the correct way. Actually, the Bible is a book of history — a book of historical science.

The Bible informs us that death entered the world after sin. This has a bearing on geology and paleontology, as the earth is covered with rocks full of fossils — dead things. Thus, the fossil-containing rocks could not have formed before sin. The Bible records the event of a global Flood — this has a great bearing on correctly interpreting the surface of the earth and the massive quantity of sedimentary rocks, as well as explaining the formation of most fossils. Of course, we have had fossils form since the Flood, but most occurred during that global event.

Now consider this: the world (through the schools and secular media) teaches that there never was a global Flood, and that death has been here since the beginning of life, eons ago. Thus, they think, the Bible's geology must be wrong!

The Bible teaches that the earth was created before the sun and it was covered with water. However, the world teaches that as a result of the "big bang," the sun came before the earth and the earth began as a hot molten body. Thus, the world thinks, the Bible's astronomy must be wrong.

The Bible teaches that God made the first man from dust, and that all people are descendants of one man — thus there is only one human race. But the world teaches that the various races of people evolved from some ape-like ancestor millions of years ago. Thus, the Bible's anthropology must be wrong, they think.

The Bible teaches that God created distinct kinds (families) of animals and plants to reproduce after their own kind. However, the world teaches that earlier animals and plants evolved into radically different kinds of creatures. Thus, they think, the Bible's biology must be wrong.

The Bible teaches that life-forms came into being, fully functioning, at the will of an infinite Creator, who must thus have also provided the code system for life (DNA and its translation machinery). The world teaches that matter by itself produced such a code system. Thus, they think, the Bible's chemistry must be wrong.

Now the history in Genesis that encompasses this geology, biology, anthropology, etc., is the same history that leads up to the message of the Cross — and out of this history come the rules (morality) by which we are to live. However, if the geology, biology, etc. are not true — then ultimately neither is the history real.

The influence of "Baconian" philosophy has progressively caused the Church to disconnect the Bible from the real world — it is relegated to a book of stories, albeit with wonderful teachings about salvation and morality.

As this thinking permeated generations of students (including those who became pastors, seminary professors, mission leaders, etc.), a "door" was pushed open further with each generation. This "door" was the one Francis Bacon had unlocked — that the Bible really has nothing to do with science. Each generation, though, became more and more consistent — if the Bible's history is not true, how can the rest of it be true? If the earthly teachings can't be trusted — how can the spiritual teachings be believed?

The result today is that increasing numbers of people no longer see the Bible as relevant, and so they reject its morality and salvation. The church is telling people, "Trust in Jesus," "abortion is wrong," "homosexual behavior is wrong," "transgender is wrong," etc., but, more and more, people don't listen because the message of Jesus and morality that the Church is preaching comes from a book that, in their minds, is not trustworthy!

This is summed up by actor Bruce Willis, who stated in a newspaper interview: "With what we know about science, anyone who thinks at all probably doesn't believe in fire and brimstone anymore. So organized religion has lost that voice to hold up their moral hand."[6]

For the Church to be successful, it needs to give up the world's false history (thus, give up "Baconian ideas") and return to the true history recorded in the Bible.

And yes, this means the Church *must* start teaching some aspects of geology, biology, anthropology, etc., in its sermons, Bible classes, youth groups, Sunday schools, and other church programs. Christians need the "big picture" of history, so that they and future generations of believers have the right foundation to correctly understand the universe and life.

Endnotes

1. Barna research online, " 'The Year's Most Intriguing Findings,' from Barna Research," https://www.christianheadlines.com/news/the-years-most-intriguing-findings-from-barna-research-1110248.html.

2. P. Johnstone and J. Mandryk, *Operation World* (GA: Paternoster, 2001), p. 747.

3. Barna research online, "Annual study reveals America is spiritually stagnant; How America's faith has changed since 9–11," August 2002; Gallup G. Jr., "Unchurched" on the rise? 15 August 15, 2002.

4. D.J. Smithwick, *Teachers, Curriculum, Control* (KY: Nehemiah Institute Inc., 1998), p. 5; Ken Ham, and Britt Beemer, *Already Gone* (Green Forest, AR: Master Books, 2009).

5. G. Barna, *Real Teens* (Ventura, CA: Regal Books, 2001), p. 136. Barna Research Online, "Teenagers embrace religion but are not excited about Christianity," August 2002.

6. Bruce Willis, actor — *Die Hard* series, *USA Weekend Magazine, Cincinnati Enquirer,* February 11–13, 2000, p. 7.

Visit the three leading, world-class Biblical attractions.

Spanning 510 feet long, this modern engineering marvel amazes visitors young and old, and **brings the Bible to life before your eyes.**

ArkEncounter.com
Williamstown, KY (south of Cincinnati)

CREATION MUSEUM.

The Creation Museum allows you to **walk through the Bible from the very beginning** using state-of-the-art exhibits and life-size animatronics.

CreationMuseum.org
Petersburg, KY (west of Cincinnati airport)

The Museum of the Bible uses innovative and cutting-edge technology that will fascinate visitors as they **experience the narrative and history of the Bible** and its impact on the world.

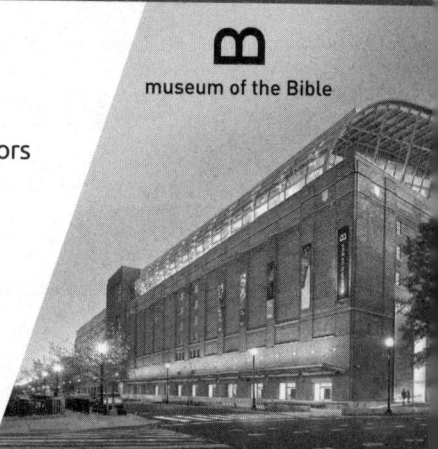

museum of the Bible

MuseumoftheBible.org
Washington, D.C.